T0209373

HEARTS ON FIRE

THE JOY OF CELEBRATING THE TRUE EASTER

ALBERT LAWRENCE

WESTBOW
PRESS®
A DIVISION OF THOMAS NELSON
& ZONDERVAN

WestBow Press books may be ordered through booksellers or by contacting:

WestBow Press
A Division of Thomas Nelson & Zondervan
1663 Liberty Drive
Bloomington, IN 47403
www.westbowpress.com
1 (866) 928-1240

ISBN: 978-1-9736-8546-3 (sc)
ISBN: 978-1-9736-8545-6 (e)

Print information available on the last page.

WestBow Press rev. date: 02/25/2020

CONTENTS

ACKNOWLEDGEMENTS

First, let me thank God Himself that by His Spirit he gave me the desire for some time to explore the meaning of the walk to Emmaus story.

I am grateful also to my family and friends who have encouraged me to keep working on this project. I am especially indebted to Mrs. Barbara Spell, an author in her own right, for helpful corrections and suggestions as the project moved forward. Thanks also goes to Mr. Steve Powell, friend and Bible teacher for his correcting and editing of the final manuscript.

I want to dedicate this book to the love of my life, Dawn Bates Lawrence, wife and best friend, without whose encouragement this book would still be on a list of projects I would like to tackle someday.

CHAPTER ONE

The Resurrection: Fact or Fable?

There is one thing that happened in human history, one event so important to all people in all cultures, in all generations that time itself was divided in half...everything that went before and everything that followed. What was it?

Was it the discovery by Columbus and by other great leaders like Galileo that the earth that the earth is round, not flat, and that it revolves around the sun, and not the other way around? Or was it perhaps the discovery and development of the internet and the high tech revolution it created all over the world?

No, it was none of the above. The answer to the question is quite simple. It was the resurrection of Jesus Christ. If that had never happened you would never have heard of the name of Jesus Christ. Everyone knew he had been put to death. Yet he was seen alive again. No one can fully explain it and no one can explain it away. It is simply true, factually true, although to many it seems too good to be true.

It is a supernatural, miraculous event, but such stories do not play well in our high- tech automated world. When people today use the word "miracle", they are usually expressing amazement concerning the latest invention.

The story of two people walking home to Emmaus, a small village seven miles from Jerusalem, is an eyewitness account given to us by Dr. Luke in his gospel account of Jesus' life and ministry. It is in the form of testimony, not parable or fable. It is about something that happened in a certain time and place. But here is what appeals to us reading it now. We can see ourselves in the two followers of Jesus walking along the road, discussing with each other what had happened to Jesus.

Who are these two followers? Luke tells us only one name: Cleopas. But who is with him? We do not have a name. Most commentaries suggest that it was a friend, perhaps his son or some other male companion and follower of Jesus. However, some people think that it was the wife of Cleopas, a woman named Mary. One prominent Biblical scholar, N.T. Wright, is in that group.

In John 19:25 we have some interesting information about some women who were present at the crucifixion. "Near the cross of Jesus stood his mother Mary, his mother's sister, Mary the wife of Clopas, and Mary Magdalene." That makes three Mary's and one unnamed woman who was the sister of the mother of Jesus.

We note that "Cleopas" was how a Greek like Luke spelled the name, whereas John, a Jew, used the Hebrew spelling, "Clopas." In addition, Cleopas urges the disguised Jesus to "stay with us" since it was getting dark. That kind of invitation would most likely come from a married couple walking to their own home. We note that they had also heard that some women had visited the tomb of Jesus and had seen Jesus alive again. This report seemed to them like utter nonsense. (Luke 24:11)

If the resurrection were a fictitious story, the author would not have included that remark. Moreover, you would not have the unrecognized Jesus calling them "foolish of heart." How would such a comment promote the story as being true? It would not. Showing the leaders as unbelieving, confused followers of Jesus would have been omitted unless that was exactly the way they were.

After the resurrection, we see changed people who had actually seen Jesus alive again with their own eyes. For example, consider the story of the conversion of a strict orthodox Jew named Saul. He was the least likely person to believe that God could or would become a human being. Yet he was the person God was soon going to change from being an enemy of the Christians to being their chief apostle.

God changed Saul's mind in a dramatic encounter as he was going on horseback to the city of Damascus, ready to arrest Christians. God struck him blind to get his attention and announce His plans, and then later healed him. This made him a thoroughly convinced eyewitness to the resurrection.

This man who was persecuting Christians and trying to stamp out their movement took on a new name: Paul. He made a complete turnaround and was converted to faith in Christ as Messiah and Lord. He still had questions about his miraculous change. He did not have answers, but in his heart he knew that there had to be answers. What he did know was enough to believe, trust and obey Jesus. God uses the same method in bringing us to faith.

If the resurrection of Jesus did not really happen, then Christianity as the Bible presents it must be false. If it is false, then Christianity is useless and so is faith in Jesus. In addition to that, those who preach Christ are false witnesses. "If Christ was not raised from the dead," Paul wrote in 1 Corinthians 15, "our faith is futile and we are still in our sins. Moreover, those who died as believers were not saved but lost." Then Paul made this bold claim for the truth of the resurrection: "If only for this life we have hope in Christ, we are to be pitied more than all men." (vs.19)

Christians would be pitied. Why? It is because we pity people who willingly believe what we know to be a lie. "But," Paul went on to say in contrast, "Christ has been raised from the dead." (1 Corinthians 15:20)

This is why, in my view, the truth about the resurrection of Christ is life's ultimate game changer, the very hinge of history. It is what

3

changed the calendar from all the years before Messiah's birth (B.C.) to all the years since then until now. (A.D.) or Anno Domini, is the Latin for "in the year of the reign of the Lord." The entire world marks its calendars from the birth of Christ.

The claim of the followers of Jesus since the first Easter is that Christ died but they saw him again with their own eyes. Christianity is based on *eyewitness testimony.* We know, of course, that eyewitness testimony is the best anyone can offer in a court of law.

John Updike, an American poet, pulls no punches when he describes the reality of the resurrected Christ. "Make no mistake: If he rose at all it was as his body. If the cells' dissolution did not reverse, the molecules reknit the amino acids rekindle, the Church will fall. It was not as the flowers each soft spring recurrent; it was not as His Spirit in the mouths and fuddled eyes of the eleven apostles. Let us not mock God with metaphor, analogy, sidestepping transcendence, making of the event a parable, a sign painted in the faded credulity of earlier ages; let us walk through the door...." [1]

The real Easter is the announcement of the seemingly incredible fact that God raised Jesus from the dead, just as He had promised. No wonder the Easter lily is a trumpet shaped flower. Trumpets sound a loud note to get our attention for some important news. In the case of Easter, the message of the hymn is clear: "Jesus Christ is risen today...Alleluia!" We hear news from ABC or CBS or CNN or Fox but this resurrection news is from another network, from heaven itself. News from God's network is never "fake." The announcers are usually angels. Hence, we have the traditional Easter greeting at worship on Easter morning

"Christ is risen!" Then the congregation answers, "He is risen, indeed! Alleluia!"

Dr. Luke, a gentile physician who became a follower of Jesus, had to have been a person with a questioning scientific mind. He says in the opening words to his gospel that he was being very careful to

---

[1] Updike, John, "Seven Stanzas at Easter, New York: Alfred A. Knopf, 20015

write "an orderly account" for letting his readers know "the certainty of the things you have been taught." (Luke 1:4)

Just think about that. We can be sure that Luke had more material to work from than only the parts we have. The information he gave us is what he regarded as the most persuasive. The three resurrection stories included in chapter 24 are those having to do with the women at the empty tomb, the walk to Emmaus, and the account of the ascension of Jesus into heaven.

The walk to Emmaus, as it has come to be known, is one of the most beloved stories in the Bible. It is about the miracle of Easter. Let us think about that walk. People in those days walked everywhere and therefore the lack of safe and reliable transportation made most people stay close to where they lived. Walking was also a much used metaphor and figure of speech in the Scriptures. Jesus promised, "Those who follow me will never walk in darkness but will have the light of life." (John 8:12) Micah the prophet said, "What does the Lord require of you? To act justly, to love mercy, and to walk humbly with your God." (Micah 6:8)

You have probably been on an Emmaus road of your own. You had hoped that the promising romance would lead to marriage, not to its breakup. You were sure that with your experience, the promotion would be offered to you, but it was not. You had hoped that your son would make good choices especially about friends, but he got involved with the wrong crowd and broke the law. You were hoping that the tests would show no cancer, but they did and while the disease seems now to be in remission, you cannot be sure that it will never return. We all know about being let down, but imagine how it felt to be let down by Jesus!

Cleopas and Mary were in no mood to hear that some women who went to Jesus' tomb to prepare his body for burial had found the tomb empty and angels inside!

> "Bowing down their faces to the ground, the angels asked, "Why do you seek the living among the dead? He is not here. He has risen. Remember how he told you while he

> was still with you in Galilee: "The Son of Man must be
> delivered into the hands of sinful men, be crucified, and
> on the third day be raised again. Then they remembered
> his words." (Luke 24:7)

However, it still seemed like nonsense. Could it be that it was intended to be read as a metaphor and figure of speech and no more than that? No. This story is about a real walk to Emmaus, an actual place seven miles west of Jerusalem, though nothing remains of it today. However, while being factual, it is quite legitimate to see it also in a figurative way. It can refer to that journey through life itself, where we believe that the risen Christ can and does walk invisibly by our side.

A Harvard professor of Psychology, Gordon Allport, was a member of my first parish in Cambridge, Massachusetts. I was not his student at Harvard where he had taught for many years, but during my time on the staff of Christ Church, (1960-66), I became his friend. He was known for his work on personality and wrote a classic textbook on that subject in the field of general and social psychology. Not everyone knew that he was also a strong believer in Jesus Christ. Those who did, both students and faculty, found it strange that he could still take Christianity seriously. However, no unbelieving professor or student would lessen Professor Allport's faithful witness to what he believed. Unlike them, he saw no conflict between psychology and Christian faith. The truth is that they are quite compatible.

One of Dr. Allport's books deals with the psychology of *rumors*. It shed some light on the reaction of those who heard about the resurrection of Jesus. He wrote that with a rumor, the story must have some importance to the speaker and the listener, and second, the facts must be shrouded in some kind of ambiguity. The ambiguity can be caused by the sketchiness of news, or some emotional tension to make the listener unwilling to accept what they heard at face value. There can be a kernel of truth in a rumor but it is usually overlaid with fanciful elaboration, making it hard to know what the underlying facts are, if any.[2]

Given the conditions under which the women went and told the disciples what they had seen and heard, we can see why the disciples dismissed their report as mere rumor. In addition, we need to realize that women in that culture were thought to be unreliable witnesses who were given to emotional displays and exaggeration. For this reason, their testimony was not allowed in courts of law. Women's rights as we know them in our day would take centuries to be recognized.

However, the fact that Dr. Luke began Chapter 24 with women having been actual witnesses to the resurrection is a clue that tells us that it must have been true. If the story were made up and not factually true then the author would never have begun his account as he did. Moreover, references to women would have made the story incredible unless, of course, it really did happen just as we are told.

Earlier in the Scriptures, the reader of the book of Job discovers that the author is revealing more than the characters in the story know. The readers know, as the characters do not, that God is testing the faith of Job by the worst of circumstances. Through the loss of everything Job has, Satan hopes to show God that Job would surely give up any faith he had. Job did not know that it was all a test, but the reader of the book does. This technique in writing is called *literary irony.* Satan is claiming that Job believed in God for selfish reasons, for the rewards God might give him. However, Job showed that his faith was a genuine trust in God no matter what tragic losses might come.

The story of the walk to Emmaus is another example of literary irony. We also know more about the news of resurrection than did Cleopas and Mary. Nothing would change the facts that they had seen Jesus die on the cross. "We *had* hoped that Jesus was going to redeem Israel." Imagine the sadness and the disappointment. Messiah was

---

[2] Allport, Gordon, The Psychology of Rumor, New York: Russell and Russell, Inc. 1947, p.33

not supposed to die like a common criminal. Therefore, Jesus seemed to them like a phony Messiah. No wonder they did not want to take some thirty minutes and walk to the tomb and see for themselves. All they wanted was to go home to Emmaus, some seven miles away, and forget how Jesus had let them down.

THE WALK WITH THE UNRECOGNIZED JESUS

As they walked along towards home, Cleopas and Mary had an animated discussion with a mysterious stranger about the cross of Jesus. Remember that they had just come from the painful experience of watching Jesus die, and with him, all their hopes for redeeming Israel and ending Roman rule. The Greek word Luke used to describe their animated conversation means: "to throw back and forth" as a tennis ball is hit back and forth across a net.

Cleopas and Mary were grief stricken, confused, depressed, and angry with God. Had you asked them, they would probably have said that the years they spent following Jesus were a waste of time. How would Jesus in disguise change their minds? If the risen Jesus had revealed his identity in some surprising way by announcing, "Here I am! It's me!" they could not have heard anything else from him. No, the shock of that approach would be just too much. He had to be disguised. The use of the passive voice is a grammatical clue to how God prevented them from full recognition prematurely. "They were kept from recognizing him."

TO RECOGNIZE MEANS, "TO KNOW AGAIN"

In my own experience, I will sometimes recognize a member of the church but he or she will not recognize me. I am out of context, not in front of the congregation dressed in clerical collar and robes. I wear my "uniform" only when it is appropriate, and I do not always have on my white, round clerical collar. I might be in a sport shirt and slacks. Appearance does affect our ability to recognize. Without my clerical collar, members of my congregation might pass me by without recognizing me.

Some years ago, the Washington Post staged an experiment in *recognition*. It was on a January morning in 2007 when Joshua Bell, a world-class violinist, stood outside a crowded Metro station in Washington, D.C. He was not dressed in the formal wear of a concert violinist but in the worn out clothing of a beggar. He had placed a hat on the floor in front of him for contributions.

What the commuters did not know was that this same musician, dressed in formal wear and holding his priceless Stradivarius violin, was playing the same music others had paid $300 a ticket to hear a few days before. Now with the same violin in hand, he is playing for the loose change people gave as they hurried to work! The hidden camera showed that more than a thousand government employees, tourists and others paid little attention to this free 45 minute performance. Joshua Bell netted $32.17 from his tips.[3]

What this shows is that *we do see what we expect to see*. Cleopas and Mary never expected to see Jesus again. He was dead and gone…or so they and everyone else thought. No wonder they did not recognize him. Common sense ruled it out. After all, they had been there watching Jesus die on the cross.

---

[3] PBS News Hour, 9/30/2014

QUESTIONS FOR REFLECTION AND DISCUSSION

1. Why can't a Christian just set aside the claims about the cross and resurrection of Jesus and just focus on his teaching? Why do Easter cards often celebrate the holiday as nothing more than a change from winter to spring?
2. Why is a miracle necessary to account for the meaning of Easter?
3. How do we learn to doubt our doubts rather than our faith in Christ?
4. Why is it true that our faith is not in our faith, nor in our feelings but on solid fact?

CHAPTER TWO

Expecting the Wrong Messiah

A s Cleopas and Mary walked along, Jesus, risen in his body but very ordinary in appearance, came up from behind and started a conversation. Jesus asked them what they were discussing. With a tone of surprise in their voices they replied,

> "Are you the only visitor to Jerusalem who doesn't know the things that have happened there in these days?" "What things?" Jesus replied. "About Jesus of Nazareth. He was a prophet, powerful in word and deed before God and all the people. The chief priests and our rulers handed him over to be sentenced to death and they crucified him. But we had hoped that he was the one who was going to redeem Israel. And what is more it is the third day since all this took place. In addition, some of our women amazed us. They went to the tomb early this morning but they did not find his body. They came and told us that they had

> seen a vision of angels, who said he was alive. Then some
> of our companions went to the tomb and found it just as
> the women had said. But him they did not see." (Luke
> 24:19-24)

Let us pause in the story to point out a detail whose meaning is easy to overlook. I find it very revealing of the character of God that in many cases *He finds us long before we find Him.* That might be you. It certainly was me. Jesus really did come looking for me prior to any interest of mine to go looking for him. The God we worship is usually taking the initiative. *He wants to be found.* He is not playing hide and seek. He can use circumstances, people, employers, friends, relatives or just anybody to start a relationship with Himself. He comes often up from behind, literally, unexpectedly, and without our awareness.

"What are you discussing together?" Jesus asked, completely unrecognized. Cleopas told him how disappointed he was that Jesus had suffered so much and was treated so badly as to wind up on a cross. Cleopas and Mary, like so many others, just could not understand how such terrible things could happen.

> "Jesus said to them "How foolish you are, and how slow
> of heart to believe all that the prophets have spoken! Did
> not the Christ have to suffer these things and then enter his
> glory? And beginning with Moses and all of the prophets
> he explained to them what was said in all the Scriptures
> concerning himself." (verses 25-27)

Notice that Jesus did not call them fools. Jesus had said in the Sermon on the Mount that anyone who says, "You fool" is in danger of the fire of hell. (Matthew 5:22) He meant that his followers are not to engage in character assassination. However, all of us have been spiritual "jerks" and "dummies" without need of taking offence. We have simply been slow to believe what the prophets said because we do not like the message. This results in our refusing to find what we are looking for. Cleopas and Mary were of that mindset. Their minds were made up. They wanted freedom and rebelling against the Romans would be the only way it could happen. Their expectations were too small and too limited to circumstances. Jesus was speaking of spiritual redemption, the inward change of the heart and mind, not a change of political and military rule.

We also remember the parable Jesus told about a foolish man. "Foolish" describes any of us who makes decisions without thinking through the consequences. For example, Jesus told the parable of the two houses, one built on sand, the other on rock. The foolish man's house was destroyed when the winds and floods came, because of the poor foundation. The wise man took more time and effort to build on rock. When the winds and storms came, the house remained intact because it was securely fastened on solid foundation. So it is with our faith in God. Not just any foundation will work.

We also need to admit to the possibility of praying selfish prayers. No ulterior motives are allowed for our own self- interest and gain. To illustrate let me quote a story which author and Manhattan pastor Tim Keller tells:

"Once upon a time there was a gardener who grew an enormous carrot. So he took it to his king and said, "My lord, this is the greatest carrot I have ever grown or ever will grow. Therefore I want to present it to you as a token of my love and respect for you." The king was touched and discerned the man's heart, so as the man turned to go, the king said, "Wait! You are clearly a good steward of the earth. I own a plot of land right next to yours. I want to give it to you as a gift so you can garden it all."

The gardener was amazed and delighted as he went home rejoicing. However, there was a nobleman at the king's court who overheard all this. And he said, "My! If that is what you get for a carrot, what if you gave the king something better?" So the next day the nobleman came before the king and as he approached he was leading a handsome black stallion. He bowed low and said, "My lord, I breed horses and this is the greatest horse I have ever bred. Therefore, I want to present it to you as a token of my love and respect." But the king discerned his heart, took the horse, and merely dismissed him. The nobleman was perplexed. The king said, "Let me explain. That gardener was giving me the carrot but you are giving yourself the horse!" [4]

How true it is. Sometimes we do unselfish things for selfish reasons. A poet named T.S. Eliot wrote: "This above all is the greatest treason, to do the right thing for the wrong reason." This is why Jesus was so critical of the Pharisees. They only appeared to be righteous to attain the approval of other people. "Be careful not to do your acts of righteousness before men, to be seen by them." (Matthew 6:1) With Jesus, motivation was just as important as activation. The "why" was just as important as the "what," and maybe more.

PREDICTION OR PROMISE?

It is important to make a careful distinction between a *prediction and a promise*. Jesus rebuked Cleopas and Mary for being "slow of heart to believe all the prophets had spoken." He did not say 'predicted.' In this context, he meant 'promised.' Meteorologists predict the weather. Nothing is personal; it is simply a matter of what nature does. Promises, however, are personal. God made special promises of blessing to those who would bless Israel, His special people. Later on, Jesus came and filled that promise fuller, in ways that surpassed the meaning of the original blessing.

Recently Dawn and I traveled back to Lancaster, PA. and to St. James' Episcopal Church where we were married 50 years ago. We invited as many of the original party of bridesmaids and groomsmen as were living and could travel back. We said the vows again. We exchanged rings again. We thought about how many and different ways those promises had been fulfilled and filled fuller from the honeymoon on through five decades.

Now imagine that at the wedding rehearsal dinner we could have seen a video prediction of what our lives would be like for the next fifty years. How do you think we would react? Would we want

---

[4] Keller, Tim, *The Prodigal God*, New York: Penguin Group, 2008, p.60

to reconsider what we were getting ourselves into and cancel the wedding? The video, you see, would include everything, the good times and the bad, the better and the worse, the richer times when we had money to pay our bills and poorer times when we had to borrow from parents to make ends meet.

The video would let us see around the corners of life and allow us to know the future which is now the past. We would be walking with Jesus to our own Emmaus, not the one that is seven miles from ancient Jerusalem, but the small town in the hill country of our own souls. We would not know who it was that unknown to us was walking beside us every day. Yes, we now know from hindsight that it was the invisible Savior who was always with us, unseen but giving us four children, twelve grandchildren, keeping promises, and answering prayers in His ways and on His schedule.

The attractive part of wanting to see it would be the hope to reverse the mistakes. However, that would not be possible. The angel showing us the video would say that nothing could be changed. That is why I would not like to have seen such a look into my future. I would always be living with a sense of "countdown" in knowing just how long I had until certain things would happen. I prefer ignorance to knowledge in a case like that. For the same reason I do not want to know the second date, the one after the dash on my grave marker. Instead, I would prefer to trust in the God who does know, but out of His love and grace spares me from knowing.

Tim Keller, author and pastor of Redeemer Presbyterian Church, New York says in his book on prayer that God is always attentive to our requests even when they are not His will. "God will either give us what we ask, or give us what we would have asked for if we knew everything He knows."[5] Keller calls this kind of praying a "restful submissiveness, a confidence that God is wiser than we are and wants the best for us." There are some prayers He has good reasons not to answer in the manner we pray. I have learned a long time ago that as

---

[5] Keller, Tim, the Prodigal God, New York: the Penguin Group, p. 18

I pray "thy kingdom come" I must also be thinking, "My kingdom *go*." Two kings cannot and will not sit on the same throne.

Cleopas and Mary had been on a wild goose chase because they were hoping for the wrong kind of Messiah. They had great expectations, but they did not know what God knew. They had missed all the clues God put into the Old Testament Scriptures. Cleopas wanted a Messiah to free them from the power of Rome; Jesus, however, wanted to be the kind of Messiah who would free them from the rule of selfishness and sin. How much greater is that freedom!

In the end of his book, the prophet Isaiah describes the human tendency to have foolish expectations. He wants us to be thinking, "How ridiculous!"

> "A man cuts down a cedar or pine tree. It is man's fuel for burning. Some of it he takes and warms himself, he kindles a fire and bakes bread. Half of the wood he burns in the fire; he roasts his meat and eats his fill. He also warms himself and says, "Ah, I am warm; I see the fire." From the rest he makes a god, his idol: No one stops to think, no one has the knowledge or understanding to say, "Half of it I used for fuel. Shall I make a detestable thing from what is left? Shall I bow down to a block of wood?" (Isaiah 44:19)

Isaiah made his illustration a mockery. However, as the old saying goes, "a rose by any other name is still a rose." We may not be prone to bow down to carved wood or sculpted stone, but we have idols nonetheless. We actually make counterfeit gods. Remember how Aaron, brother of Moses, dealt with the impatience of waiting for Moses to come back from his mountain retreat where God gave the Ten Commandments? The people collected gold jewelry, melted it down and fashioned a large golden calf. Then they had the audacity to worship it and treat it as a substitute for the real God. While golden calves do not relate to modern Americans, yet the issue is timeless.

Tim Keller writes, "A counterfeit god is anything that is so central and essential to your life, that should you lose it, your life would feel hardly worth living." Idols can actually be made of good things. It might be your spouse, your family, your career, or your achievements. It can be a romantic relationship, your beauty, your approval by your peers, your success, your popularity, your possessions, your position, your power, your craving of luxury, etc. "An idol is whatever you look at and say, "If I could just have that, then I will know my life has meaning, value and real significance." [6]

I thought about this on a recent drive to Houston on Interstate 45. Just before reaching the city, all traffic has to go under an overhead railroad bridge. On the side visible to all drivers is some graffiti painted white in large letters. The graffiti is just two words: BE SOMEBODY. Those two words summarize what some people say is the main problem with our culture. Nobody wants to be a nobody. Yet the main message of the gospel of Jesus Christ is that everyone who believes IS already a somebody. They have all the acceptance and approval they need. Our preaching, teaching and missionary work should focus on meeting this need, whether or not it is phrased in those two words.

Certainly, this means that Jesus knew the plan of salvation and what benefit would accrue to all his followers when they were able to experience forgiveness of their sins and the promise of eternal life. He knew that his resurrection was coming with its glorious outcome. That is what would make him able to endure the terrible suffering and dying.

> "Let us fix our eyes on Jesus, the author and perfecter of
> our faith, who for the joy set before him, endured the cross,
> scorning its shame, and sat down at the right hand of the
> throne of God." (Hebrews 12:2)

But why did Jesus choose Cleopas and Mary for this fascinating story of the walk to Emmaus? If you were Jesus, wouldn't you want to appear to Pontius Pilate, or to a gathering of Pharisees? How about

---

[6] Ibid. p.xviii

appearing to the high priest or to the Roman Emperor? No, God had his reasons. Perhaps He chose Cleopas and Mary because they were among the few followers who were watching Jesus die. They saw the nails pounded into his wrist. They saw the cross erected upright and the blood that flowed from the wounds. They saw Jesus' mother hold the body. Then they all went home to wait out the coming Sabbath day when work had to stop. After the Sabbath was over, they were free to travel home again.

They were so preoccupied with his death that on Sunday when some women who had been to the tomb first came back and said Jesus was alive, Cleopas and Mary dismissed the words as nonsense. They did not even bother to spend another thirty minutes to go and check it out for themselves. They got packed and starting walking away from, not towards the tomb. They were not expecting the miracle of resurrection. It was going to be the greatest surprise anyone could ever have imagined. No, Jesus was making a point in selecting ordinary "nobodies" to become his followers. Think about the twelve disciples. Think how Jesus redefined greatness and had to deal with skewed ideas about it in his own disciples, James, and John. He redefined greatness as God sees it, not as the culture defines it.

> "Whoever wants to become great among you must become your servant, and whoever wants to be first must be slave of all. For even the Son of man did not come to be served but to serve, and give his life a ransom for many." (Matthew 20:28)

Jesus rebuked Cleopas and Mary for being "*slow of heart to believe all that the prophets have spoken*." Note that word "spoken." Prophets are those people whom God singles out to be His representatives. What the prophets speak is no more and no less and nothing else but what they hear God say. Prophets are the mouthpieces for God. Believing means not only agreeing that God's truth is credible but that it is believable and life changing. "Trust and obey" is not just the title of a song. It is sound advice.

With children sometimes I use a simple analogy to help them to see the true meaning of following Jesus. "Three frogs were sitting on a log. One frog decided to jump off the log. So how many frogs are now on the log?" Usually they will say "two." I reply that "there are still three on the log. I did not say that any frog jumped, but that only that one frog *decided* to jump." He did not carry through with his decision. Neither can we become log sitters and remain there. Not to decide is in itself a decision by default. A spinning coin will not keep on spinning long. It will come down either heads or tails. Default outcomes are usually not the best. Just as the coin will have only two outcomes, so it is with us. Either we will want to know and do the truth as Jesus explains it, or we will want him to see things as we do and act accordingly. This was the case with Cleopas and Mary.

I have met people like them in parish ministry. They are slow to believe and to let their knowledge of Scripture make any difference in their behavior. I am thinking of someone who was reading at worship one of the "hard sayings" of Jesus. He ended with the usual, "This is the word of God." Then after a brief pause, he added, "Unfortunately!" Obviously, the reader did not like what Jesus said.

In just that one word he preached a sermon. God's word is *God's* word. We cannot soften it, add to it or subtract from it. We accept it as His unchanging truth, like it or not. There is no need to update it or upgrade it because it cannot be done. "I am the Lord I do not change."(Malachi 3:6) When it comes to God's word written, you can doubt it; you can disbelieve it; you can like it; you can dislike it; but you cannot change it.

QUESTIONS FOR DISCUSSION AND REFLECTION

1. Do you pray unselfish prayers selfishly without knowing it?
2. How do you tell a prediction from a promise?
3. How do we make good things into counterfeit gods?
4. Why is it so easy to decide but so hard to put prayers into action?

CHAPTER THREE

The Authority of Scripture

One of the most puzzling traits of our 21st century culture is the growing tendency among younger Americans to resist any kind of authority. Preferences and choices are now in vogue. Relativism is in style. Opinions are all equally valid. Truth is not discovered; it is invented and custom tailored to our wishes. Feelings are given as much weight as reason. Authority is made up as we go along. This kind of Alice in Wonderland world, however, is unreal and dangerous.

For example, when we are driving and we notice a police officer directing traffic at the coming intersection what do we see? We see a human just like us but with one great difference. He has authority given to him by the federal government, the state, or the county, an authority which drivers must respect and obey. The police officer can put up his hand and everyone must come to a stop. We see the gun, we see the uniform, and we see the shiny badge. We recognize and accept their authority. If we are driving and they signal for us to pull over, we obey.

I remember the time when I was driving through a small town and a police officer stopped me. It was about nine p.m. After I produced the driver's license and insurance card, I asked what the problem was. He replied, "You had your lights on high beam when you were on a two lane road." Then, as he returned my license and registration cards, he said, "Be more careful and not make it hard on other drivers to see oncoming traffic." Authority is authority, regardless of how important or trivial the issue may seem.

True authority is something we receive. It is a given thing. We have no permission to pick the laws we want to obey. It is not about choosing or preferring.

Not long ago I was having work done on my teeth. My dentist is a strong believer and we got into a discussion about the Bible. His daughter had enrolled in a college course entitled, "The Bible as Literature." While it is true that the Bible is literature, it is not less than that, but it is so much more. Nonetheless, the teacher felt that students needed to know that they would be reading the Bible as only literature, not theology. They were to think of God as just another character in the story, no different from any other person.

Is this possible? No. My dentist and I agreed that his daughter needed to drop the course. She did. Moreover, she was wise in doing so.

In contrast to what that English professor said, here is how St. Paul regarded Scripture:

> "We also thank God continually because when you received the word of God, which you heard from us, you accepted it not as the word of men, but as it actually is, the word of God, which is at work in you who believe." (I Thessalonians 2:13)

I want you to notice several points that are relevant to our study here: First, Paul mentions that the word of God *is received.* Picture a delivery being made to you by UPS or FedEx or USPS.

Someone comes to your door and hands you a package. Your name is written on the front. You *receive* it and perhaps sign for it as having been delivered. As you open it you see gift wrapping. This means you *accept* it when you open and find out it is something delivered for you and you only, and that a friend or relative sends it. Someone was thoughtful, loving, and wanted to express feelings of love and appreciation. Moreover, you and I receive and accept the gospel, the good news of Jesus Christ, in the same way.

I want you to notice something else about Scripture according to Paul. It is the word of God, which IS at work in you who believe. Notice the grammar here. The word of God, the Scripture, is described in the *present tense.* It is never expired or outdated.

The Scriptures, to be sure, do contain lots of history of the Jewish people, as Cleopas and Mary knew. Yet they were "slow of heart to believe all that the prophets had spoken." Their concept of what God should and should not do with His people was for their benefit. Jesus was helping them to see that. However, Cleopas and Mary may have thought that the Scriptures applied to problems and issues of ancient times, but not their present world, not to a culture like theirs. The New Testament had not yet been written, but Jesus must have detected their habit of seeing Scripture through a *historical* lens only. What could Moses and the prophets know about Roman tyranny? That is the difference between the Scriptures and any other literature. God continues to speak through what He has already spoken, even long ago in the ancient world.

> Secondly, Paul wrote, "the Word of God *is living and active.* Sharper than any double edged sword, it penetrates even to dividing soul and spirit, joints and marrow; it judges the thoughts and attitudes of the heart." (Hebrews 4:12)

There are no new sins and no new virtues. Every generation has to deal with Adam's problem of sin. It comes standard at our birth. We do not get to modify our genes. It is in our spiritual DNA. This is why the Scripture is the *only book that reads you even as you read it!* Soren Kierkegaard, the Danish author wrote, "the truth is a snare; you cannot have it without being caught. You cannot have the truth in such a way that you catch it, but only in such a way that it catches you."[7]

What a privilege it was for Cleopas and Mary to hear from Jesus that he, Jesus, called himself the personification of truth and the subject of ALL of the Scripture, even the first or "Old" Testament. Jesus pointed out that all through the history of the Jewish people God was dropping hints and clues that became a theme when connected to each other. One prophecy was added to another, each showing the trajectory of God's purpose with His people, fulfilling and filling fuller the promises He made.

THE LESSON OF THE MAYONNAISE JAR

One day a history professor stood before his class with a large jar and several items in front of him. When the class began, without saying a word, he picked up an extra-large mayonnaise jar and filled it with golf balls. He then asked the students if the jar was full. They said it was full. The professor then picked up a box of pebbles and poured them into the jar. He shook the jar and the pebbles rolled into the open areas between the golf balls. He then asked the students if it was truly full. They agreed that it was.

Next, the professor picked up a box of sand and poured it into the jar. Of course, the sand filled up every space remaining. Again, he asked if the jar was full. They all said yes. Next, he produced two cups of coffee from underneath his desk, and poured them into the jar. The students laughed. "Now," said the professor, "I want you

---

[7] Kierkegaard, Soren as quoted in Os Guinness, Long Journey Home, Colorado Springs, CO, Waterbrook Press, 2001 p.204

to recognize that this jar represents your life. The golf balls stand for the important things such as God, family, work, and friends. If everything else in your life was lost and only they remained, your life would still be full. The pebbles stand for the small stuff. If you put the sand into the jar first, then there is no room for the golf balls and the pebbles together. Therefore, if you spend all your time on small stuff you will never make time for the important things.

Therefore, we see that having one promise, but different levels of fulfillment, is something we find in our own human experience.

THE LESSON OF THE GRADUATION GIFT

Here is another example: Suppose a father living in the 1970's promised his high school senior son a new electric typewriter for use in college. Meanwhile, however, the computer age was dawning and there was a new kind of typewriter called the word processor. It was still a typewriter but with new amenities such as the delete button. There would be no messy erasing. There were many kinds and sizes of fonts, plus new ways of storing and retrieving saved documents.

Did the father renege on his promise to his son by giving him a word processor instead of a typewriter? No, he kept the promise and more, in a way that exceeds what he first announced. The same purpose is behind the two statements, but the computer surpasses what even the latest and best typewriter would be able to do. The promise was made in terms of what was available at the time; but it was filled and filled fuller later by a vastly improved invention. In the same way, God kept his original promise to Abraham and his descendants. As generations came and went, and historical events made a few people into a great nation of believers, the promise was filled fuller at a new and higher level.

This analogy helps us to understand the meaning of the mountain top vision we call the Transfiguration of Jesus. (Matthew 17) In this vision, Jesus appears to the disciples in dazzling white apparel with two great leaders from the past, Moses and Elijah. We are told that they are discussing together the "exodus" which Jesus would accomplish for his people in Jerusalem. It was to be a new and more glorious experience than the famous exodus from Egypt under Moses. Even though it would involve for Jesus intense suffering, a cruel and unjust death, there would follow an unheard of event, the resurrection of Jesus from the dead.

The three persons in the vision, Moses, Elijah and Jesus, were all used by God to bring freedom from oppression. Moses brought the Jews out of Egypt and from the bondage under Pharaoh, king of Egypt. Elijah was first in the line of prophets who would challenge His people to make up their mind and not divide their allegiance between God and the pagan deity named Baal. However, it was Jesus who would lead them to a new "exodus." Jesus would bring the greatest of all freedoms, the undeserved pardon of sins. Jesus would provide the ultimate sacrifice of himself on the cross, taking our place and dying our death as full payment for our sin against a holy God. That is why we say that the gospel is not advice from Jesus. It is news like no other news bulletin anyone has ever heard. The essence of it is this:

> *There is no good thing you can do to make God love you more.*

> *There is no bad thing you can do to make God love you less.*

On the cross one of the last things Jesus said was "It is finished." He did not "*I* am finished" but "*it* is finished." What does "it" refer to? It refers to his mission. It is the reason he came into the world.

> "This is a true saying and worthy of all men to be received, that Christ Jesus came into the world to save sinners." (1 Timothy1:15)

WHO ARE THESE SINNERS? ANSWER:
EVERYONE IS A SINNER

Sadly, it is hard to commend the Bible's inherent authority to the present generation. This is due to the popularity of a worldview where no one submits to anybody at all. However, the words ought and must are words that are not questioned by those same people if they are serving in the military. You can disobey an order, they say, but only once. Consequences teach you that. Of course, the enlistment department makes sure that you promise to obey your superior officers without question or hesitation.

Others in our culture think that decisions should not be made by command, but by *preference and choice*. When it comes to accepting the authority of Scripture, we need to remember that this is not an order we must obey but a choice that allows us to live life as God created it. For example, it seems reasonable to anyone who wants to follow Jesus that a disciple needs to "buy into" the mindset of the person being followed. If Jesus himself is submitted to the authority of Scripture then so any follower must also be submitted in the same way. Here is one definition Tallowood Baptist Church, Houston, adopted in its mission statement: "A disciple of Jesus Christ follows him, learns from him, lives like him, and leads others to do the same." So much is said in so few words.

Jesus illustrates this clearly in a case where a Roman army officer with a centurion, with a hundred men in his command, had a servant suffering from paralysis and in great pain. He had heard that Jesus had remarkable powers of healing that are available even to outsiders like him. He went to Jesus and explained his need.

> Jesus said, "I will go and heal him." The centurion replied, "Lord, I do not deserve to have you come under my roof. But just say the word, and my servant will be healed. For I am a man under authority with soldiers under me. I tell this one "go" and he goes, and that one "come" and he comes. I say to my servant, "Do this" and he does

---

it." When Jesus heard this he was astonished and said to those following him, "I tell you the truth, I have not found anyone in Israel with such great faith. Go, it will be done as you believed it would." (Matthew 8:5)

Do you see what this encounter says about authority? It says that faith is the foundation. Faith is based on the trust we place in the character of God who stands behind what He says. If we want great faith we must learn that it is not how much we know about God, for the centurion knew very little. But he knew that all the power of the Roman government was backing a simple command. Likewise, he believed that behind the words of Jesus stands all the authority of Almighty God who made heaven and earth. God Himself with all His power and wisdom come through the words of Jesus.

JESUS OPENS THE SCRIPTURES

There are many statements in the Old Testament that Jesus could have chosen to explain. To the ordinary mind, the cross looked like the greatest miscarriage of justice in all of history. However, the cross was not what it appeared to be, but so much more. God wrote the cross into the script for our salvation. This itself was ironic since the Romans prided themselves in being a people whose government is built on justice. In their eyes, a cross was both a deserved punishment and a deterrent to criminal behavior. This begs the question of who actually killed Jesus. The answer is not obvious.

WHO KILLED JESUS?

Can we believe it was the Roman colonial governor, Pontius Pilate, who gave the order to crucify? Or was it the Roman soldiers who carried it out? How about the scheming, jealous religious leaders? Yes, it was all of those. How could God let such injustice happen? It is

27

because He wanted to. He was using evil to defeat evil, paradoxical as that might sound.

Mel Gibson, in the movie he made in 2005, The Passion of the Christ, broke some long established movie making rules. For example, we are told that the hand, which held the spike as it went through the wrist of Jesus, was Mel Gibson's hand. In addition, when Mary was given the body of Christ she looked at Jesus and then, staring into the lens of the camera, looked directly into it and to us in the audience. It was as if to say, "You out there, watching. You had a part in this also."

Mary was right. Jesus really did die for OUR sins, yours and mine and for the sins of the entire world. He died for those who were looking forward to the Savior to come, as well as for all those like you and me who look back on it some 2100 years later. That haunting question in the Christian hymn, "Were you there?" is easy to answer. "Yes, we *were* there. He took our place. His cross was my cross, and yours as well. He was our substitute, dying our death, paying our sin debt in full, crediting our spiritual account with the righteous of Jesus. It was a righteousness we could never have earned or deserved."

There is a famous painting by Rembrandt called, "The Raising of the Cross." It shows several soldiers lifting the cross into place. One of them looks exactly like Rembrandt because it is actually a self-portrait. There he is with his large hat with the feather sticking out, and he is taking the part of a Roman soldier. Therefore, Rembrandt was saying with his paintbrush that he too killed Jesus. So did the apostle Paul, who wrote, "While we were yet sinners Christ died for us." (Romans 5:6)

THE APOSTLE PAUL SPOKE FOR US ALL IN WRITING THIS CONFESSION:

"For I do not understand what I do. For what I want to do, I do not do, but what I hate I do. And if I do what I do not want to do, I agree that the law is good. As it is, it is no longer I myself who do it, but it is sin living in me. I know that nothing good lives in me, that is, in my sinful nature. For I have the desire to do what is good, but I cannot carry it out. For what I do is not the good I want to do; no, the evil I do not want to do, this I keep on doing."(Romans 7:15-20)

Paul calls this dilemma a battle between two laws:[8]

"This law of sin wages war against the law of my mind, making me a prisoner of the law of sin at work within my members." (Romans 7:23)

This is everyone's battle and struggle. It is a battle we need to fight and with God's help, to win. Paul wonders to himself if anyone will rescue him from what he calls "this body of death." Then it dawns on him. God did rescue him and will rescue him again. "Thanks be to God, through Jesus Christ our Lord." (Romans 8:1)

When you think of why God visited this planet in the person of His son Jesus, do you think it was perhaps for learning firsthand how human beings are doing? No, God does not need human beings as reporters. He needs no one to inform Him. As Anglicans say in opening a service of worship:

"Almighty God, unto whom all hearts are open, all desires known, and from whom no secrets are hid, cleanse the thoughts of our hearts by the inspiration of your Holy Spirit, that we may perfectly love you and worthily magnify your holy name."

No, the cross was in the script of God's plan for saving us from ourselves. It came as no surprise, as we learn clearly from the account of Jesus' praying in the Garden of Gethsemane just before his arrest. The cross was going to be the means whereby God could acquit the guilty because Jesus had already paid everyone's penalty both on their behalf and in their place. The word for this exchange is substitution. "The essence of sin is man substituting himself for God, while the

---

[8] Stott, John, The Cross of Christ, Leicester, England, Inter Varsity Press, 1984 p. 160

essence of salvation is God substituting himself for man. Man asserts himself against God and puts himself where God deserves to be; God sacrifices himself for man and puts himself where only man deserves to be. Man claims prerogatives which belong to God alone; God accepts penalties which belong to man alone."[9]

QUESTIONS FOR THOUGHT AND DISCUSSION

1. Why do you think that the younger generation has a problem with accepting authority?
2. What can help us see that Jesus' death and resurrection was an accomplishment? What was accomplished?
3. How does the cross and resurrection fit into the unity of the whole Bible?
4. How are you and I guilty of killing Jesus?
5. Read Romans 7. Does every human being have this inner battle going on?

---

[9] Stott, Ibid., p. 160

CHAPTER FOUR

God Knows Best

We begin this chapter with a statement of what made Cleopas and Mary so disappointed and sad. The object of their hope was not worthy of their trust. To put it simply, they backed the wrong horse! In fact, their "horse" was not in the race. Their expectations, though great, were contrary to God's decided plans. They thought that a change of government was the answer. However, this was really an example of a solution looking for a problem. What they learned by the end of their walk with Jesus is the truth that HE was the answer to a problem much bigger than who was governing Israel.

Thinking that God sees things as we do is a common assumption in every generation of believers. Yes, Jesus did say that we are to ask in a believing heart and God will answer our prayer. Praying in Jesus' name, however, is not a claim on his generosity or a guarantee of anything. We cannot pray just anything in Jesus' name. God will hear that prayer if it conforms to His will as well as ours. Without that match of wills and motivations, we could easily find ourselves asking God to act contrary to His nature. We always need to keep in mind that to pray in Christ's name is to place a filter in front of our words. Haven't you been relieved that looking back on the past, some of your prayers were not granted? Remember that "no" is a real answer. Sometimes we find ourselves thanking God that He did not answer as we expected.

For example, in my own life, I was interested as a teenager in all things having to do with electronics. I thought it might lead to a career as an electrical engineer. God had His way of saying no to that idea. He first allowed me admission in the College of Engineering at University of Maryland. However, as I took various required courses I did poorly in higher math. However, hindsight, which is always after the fact, made my humiliation a positive direction from the Lord. I then realized that I needed to meet with a counselor whose specialty was to help students make good career choices.

I changed majors and enrolled in the College of Arts and Sciences in order to find some new career path geared to talent, not interest. Considering all the possibilities and after some educational testing, the teaching profession seemed like a good fit. I changed to the University's College of Education and did well in preparation to teach French language and literature. I looked forward to helping high school students to succeed in a difficult subject required for graduation.

However, God was again directing me, seemingly by a process of elimination. I was to teach, all right, but not a foreign language. It would be the teaching of the good news of God's salvation in Jesus Christ, a subject that makes an eternal difference in the lives of people. I would teach how to have a personal trust relationship with God by introducing them to the Scriptures and to the person of Jesus Christ. God caused a number of events to happen including what seemed like a chance meeting with people of great faith. They asked me to come to a Bible study and see how the Bible gave me a proven way to know what God was calling me to do with my life.

As time went by, I became active in a local congregation where several pastors were inspiring examples of the work of full time ordained ministry. With their help, I explored the requirements for a career in the ordained ministry. That meant enrolling in a three-year course of studies at a theological seminary. Looking back across the years from more than 50 years of service, I see how God had used many people and varied circumstances to make His will clear.

Cleopas and Mary had their own great expectations, but the expectations were not in God's will, nor were they great as those God had for them. They had simply decided in advance that of course God would want to free them from their hard life under the Roman occupation. Why would He not? However, they were dictating to God, not praying for His will. They wanted God to bring back glory days of old. Nothing was wrong with those wishes except that God had a much bigger and better kind of redemption than that. God was not about to send a Superman to the rescue. He would come to the rescue Himself, but His enemy would be much harder to conquer than any foreign government. The enemy God was going to conquer was Satan himself. God's coming as Messiah would be the undoing of Satan as well as death itself. God would come to conquer sin and death and to provide believers a way to freedom from the consequences.

C. S. Lewis, the great teacher and author in the last century, may have oversimplified somewhat, but his words are a kind of wake-up call for anyone. "There are two kinds of people in the world; those who say to God, "Thy will be done" and those to whom God says, "All right, have it your way. Your will be done."[10]

What Lewis means is that God does not force anyone to choose His way. He respects the freedom to choose which He gave every human being. We are not animals doing what comes by way of instinct. We are made in His image, meaning that we have the privilege of being able to reason before making conscious decisions. We have a built in truth and lie detector we call "conscience." Yet, even though we may

---

[10] www.goodreads.com/quotes/733731

know what the right and the good and the true things are, we have a default tendency to put self first.

Jesus would suffer and die vicariously, not for any sins of his own for he had none. He would die in our place, in our stead. His mercy would be in NOT giving us the penalty *He do deserve.* By His grace, we would give us the forgiveness we *do not deserve.* The cross would be the only way for this reconciliation with humanity to be possible. Only a sinless human being could make atonement in the eyes of a holy God. Only Jesus could qualify.

As the walk to Emmaus continued, Jesus pretended to be totally uninformed. He knew exactly what was on their minds and how he was the main character in the story of the cross. However, he wanted to know how these two disciples were dealing with the puzzling facts of the past week. "What things?" the unrecognized and disguised Jesus asked, knowing full well what was on Cleopas and Mary's mind. They replied,

> "Are you only a visitor to Jerusalem and do not know the things that happened there in these days?" "What things?" Jesus asked. "About Jesus of Nazareth," they replied. "We had hoped that he was going to redeem Israel but our chief priests and rulers handed him over to be sentenced to death and they crucified him." (Luke 24:19, 21)

It was not the first time that a follower of Jesus revealed total confusion over why the cross was necessary. Perhaps Cleopas and Mary were once standing within earshot of the heated conversation Jesus had with Peter about the cross.

> Jesus "explained to his disciples that he must go to Jerusalem and suffer many things at the hands of the elders, chief priests and teachers of the law, and that he must be killed and on the third day be raised to life." (Luke 24:45)

Peter simply meant to show his loyalty when he replied, "Never! This shall never happen to you." Nevertheless, how ridiculous was the thought that Peter could personally protect Jesus from any harm! Not only was it insulting of Peter to think that his master had it all wrong. After all, who is wiser here? Who is the teacher and who is the pupil? Maybe Peter forgot that lesson Jesus taught one day about a servant and his master:

> "A student is not above his teacher, nor a servant above his master. It is enough for the student to be like his teacher, and the servant like his master."(Matthew 10:24)

The prophet Isaiah had said virtually the same thing centuries before:

> "Who has understood the mind of the Lord or instructed him as his counselor? Whom did the Lord consult to enlighten him, or who taught him the right way? Who was it that taught him knowledge or showed him the path of understanding?" (Isaiah 40:14)

It seems ridiculous. Yet so often, we do just that. We bring our wishes and plans before the Lord and instead of asking Him to change them according to His will, we simply put in our orders. However, He is not a spiritual 'Amazon" internet provider. Or we dismiss what we know is the right thing to do, and what is consistent with Bible teaching, because we don't like it. What we can learn is that God's will is always best, whether or not we understand it or approve it. The emblem of Nike products on sportswear would also be a great motto for Christians: "Just Do It."

Think back now on the fervent prayers you may have prayed in the past that remained unanswered. You may have prayed so hard that the woman or man you were dating would want to continue but you broke up. Later you met a much better potential spouse and you were relieved that you were able to wait. In addition, how about that promotion you did not get at work? Someone else less deserving got it instead. What you did not know is that a better offer would be coming to you from another company only a short time later. That was the silver lining behind the cloud. We cannot see around corners, but God can. This is why we, like Cleopas and Mary, are apt to think that God let us down. God, however, never fails in what He does, even though it may seem that way to us.

Jesus said that Cleopas and Mary were "foolish and slow to believe all that the prophets have spoken." If they had understood Scripture, they would have known that God's prophets might be unpopular but they are always right.

Yet there is much more that motivates Jesus to say that Cleopas and Mary were *foolish and slow to believe the prophets*. What was it? They rated political and military power over the power of God. The end of Roman tyranny was a good thing but they thought that it was the best thing. *They simply wanted something from God more than they wanted God Himself.*

C. S. Lewis said that all of us have this inclination to some degree. We put second things first. Not long ago Dawn and I attended a service in which the preacher was expounding this point. As we left the worship an usher handed us a wristband with the words I AM SECOND on it. Everyone needs to remember that.

Lewis wrote, "Every preference of a small good to a great, or partial good to a total good, involves the loss of the small or partial good for which the sacrifice is made. You cannot get second things by putting them first. You get second things only by putting first things first."[11] It is a paradox, but it is true nonetheless.

Lewis further explained this principle of overvaluing a lesser good resulting in the loss of it. "Put first things first and we get second things thrown in; put second things first and we lose both first and second things." Jesus said as much when he warned against making anything else but God our real treasure. The root problem is elevating things above our love for God. It is believing that something else

[11] Lewis, C.S. God in the Dock, Grand Rapids, Michigan: Eerdmanns, 1970, p. 278

but faith in God will be the answer to our search for contentment. I thought of this one day as I noticed that the car in front of me, a pricey sports car, framed the license plate with a metal bracket. On the bracket were the words, "crave luxury."

That begs the question, "what do we think will make us happy and satisfied?" For Cleopas and Mary they let Jesus know that "we had hoped that (Messiah) would be the one to redeem Israel." Both of them felt let down, just because God did not rubber stamp their own solution to their problem. What they should have done was to pray to God and ask if their program was or was not in His will. In other words, they needed to love their plan less than they loved God. The word for that is to relinquish, to let go of, and surrender.

The odd and truly paradoxical truth is that when we put anything first, even a good thing, and make it our treasure instead of God, we have made it into an idol. A friend of mine let himself become grossly overweight and obese until his appetite for food overruled his common sense. He said to me in a nonchalant way, "It is because I love to eat." He did not know or care about moderation. He let his stomach rule. He said, "I love chocolate and bacon, but they are the cocaine of any diet." He found out the hard way how foolish it is to draw too much enjoyment from eating. In the end, he lost his enjoyment of food and became its slave instead. It took more and more food to get his previous good feeling through it. The very thing that he thought would give him pleasure ended up being the problem itself.

The principle holds true; the best way to destroy our enjoyment of a good thing is to make it *the main thing*. It could be career, spouse, children, reputation, sex, money, power, possessions, position, hobby, etc. It is the same principle. Put any good God given pleasure in place of God Himself and you lose them both.

"IN ALL THE SCRIPTURES THE THINGS ABOUT HIMSELF."

Remember that the scrolls of the Old Testament, or First Testament, were the only Scriptures Jesus had. Jesus made a claim that even though thirty-nine authors composed the Old Testament over thousands of years, it was *all about him!* Think about what that claim assumes. It is a claim to be God.

Sometimes it seems as though God were staging a scavenger hunt in the Scriptures. He is leaving clues here and there, some verses pointing directly to Christ, as we find in the prophet Isaiah, but others more obliquely. It takes careful study to find all the clues, but the truth remains; *God wants to be found even more than we want to find Him.* When we say that we have found Christ, what we mean is that He has found us and we have said yes to his call to follow him.

Believing that has kept many people hunting until at last, they find the treasure of knowing God in Jesus Christ. The things that had happened during that last week before Easter were in the mind of the Father since time began. God was not winging it, not making up His plan as time went by, and as circumstances changed. He was never "under the circumstances" but the one who is above them and never surprised by anything. He was always in control, and still is. The Scriptures build upon themselves like chapters in a mystery novel. The cross and resurrection are the climax and final fulfillment of all the promises of God. This is how we are to understand the relation between Old and New Testaments.

Think of promises made in the Old Testament and promises fulfilled in the New Testament.

> "Blessed are your eyes, for they see, and your ears for they hear. Truly I say to you, many prophets and righteous men longed to see what you see and did not see it, and to hear what you hear and did not hear it. (Matthew13:16, 17)

This is why we are not to think of the Old Testament as an old car that needs replacing. The New Testament does not abrogate the Old, nor is there any need for updating or upgrading.

Jesus says, "Heaven and earth shall pass away but my words shall not pass away." (Luke 21:33) There really is something that lasts forever. It is God's Word written.

QUESTIONS FOR THOUGHT AND DISCUSSION

1. What is the correct way of distinguishing between the Old and New Testaments?
2. How is it true that sometimes we use God or try to keep Him on retainer as we might do with a financial or legal counselor?
3. Can you cite times when you have allowed a good thing to become the main thing?
4. What will remind us to want God more than anything we want from God?

CHAPTER FIVE

The Things That Happened

Palm Sunday

The Sunday of Holy Week was what today we would call a "demonstration." Jesus rode into the city of Jerusalem where crowds had gathered for the annual feast of Passover. Jesus did not want to enter the city and receive what might have become a royal welcome. He had no intention to become that kind of king. There were many who, like Cleopas and Mary, regarded him as the Messiah sent by God to throw off the yoke of the Roman occupation. Jesus, not Caesar, was their Lord.

Therefore, Jesus borrowed a donkey from a secret follower. By choosing such an animal instead of a white horse, he would be riding on the American equivalent of an old pick-up truck. His choice of transportation announced that he did not want a royal treatment. He did not want the welcome of a conqueror coming off a great victory, with trumpets sounding and soldiers marching. In that case, he would be on a white horse in full dress uniform and with perhaps a few defeated enemy officers walking behind in chains.

His followers were numerous, and some of them expressed their feelings by spreading palm branches in front of the donkey, while others put their cloaks on the road. It was a kind of "red carpet" welcome. Others were shouting, "Blessed is he who comes in the name of the Lord. Blessed is the kingdom of our father David. Hosanna in the highest." The better life during David's reign many years earlier was on their mind.

Matthew notes that the" whole city was stirred, asking, "Who is this?" Others answered with simple data. "This is Jesus, the prophet from Nazareth in Galilee." (Matthew.21:11) Name, address, occupation. True, but how much more needs to be said about who Jesus is.

THE CLEANSING OF THE TEMPLE

The second of the "things" that happened during "Holy Week" was the cleansing of the Temple. Jesus entered the Temple area and acted as if he owned the place (which in fact he did). He was so deeply hurt and aggravated to see all the corruption and commercialism. Money changers were taking big profits for exchanging Roman money for the special currency acceptable for use in the temple. Sellers of lambs needed for sacrifice charged high prices and took great profits.

In true righteous indignation, Jesus overturned the tables of the moneychangers and the benches of those selling sacrificial doves.

> "It is written," he said in a loud voice, "My house will be called a house of prayer but you are making it a 'den of robbers.'"

Jesus was the true reformer. But his reform was unwanted and it is unwanted now for the same reason.

41

THE MOUNT OF TRANSFIGURATION.
THE OLD PASSOVER AND THE NEW "EXODUS"

From childhood, Jesus would come to Jerusalem with his family each year to celebrate Moses' great rescue mission known as the Passover. It is a special remembrance of the time when God punished the king of Egypt, Pharaoh, because he refused to let the Jews go free. Today we would call such punishing acts *"sanctions."* These were intended by God to be so painful to the Pharaoh that he would change his mind and let the Jewish people be free from slavery. The worst of these sanctions was the death of all the firstborn in the land, along with animals and people, the Pharaoh's own family included.

On that terrible night when the angel of death carried out God's plan, His own people were spared in a unique way. Each family would need to kill a lamb and put its blood on the doorposts to let the death angel know that God's people lived inside. Then the angel would 'pass over' that home. They were under the provision of a lamb whose blood was shed instead of the first born in the family. This act foreshadowed the sacrifice of the "Lamb of God who takes away the sins of the world," namely Jesus.

God told them to remember this turning point in the story of their history with a special meal. Deuteronomy 26 gives the text. Unleavened bread would remind them of the rush to escape with no time to allow leaven to rise in the bread. Bitter herbs would remind them of their bitter life as slaves. The cups of wine would serve to recall the joyful feeling of knowing that God had set them free with no help from them. It was a pure gift of His grace. The laws of God had not yet been given.

Sometimes we forget that *grace came before law,* as the apostle Paul would thoroughly explain in his letters. We keep the law of God not to get something we might deserve, but to give thanks for God's undeserved gift of His forgiveness in Christ. Obeying the laws of God would come from gratitude for God's grace, not desire to earn or deserve it. Jesus showed his divine authority by changing the Passover script! He simply broke the bread and said, "This is my

HEARTS ON FIRE

body, given for you". Then he took the cup and said, "This cup is my blood of the new covenant which is poured out for many."

Notice the words "new covenant." Jesus was connecting the original Passover with a new one. He was saying that the deliverance from Egypt under Moses was not an ending but another chapter in a continuing work of God. It was pointing to the Savior when the sacrificial lamb would not be an animal but a human being, someone who would be no less than God in human form. He would be a person whose death would be the ultimate vicarious sacrifice that takes away the sins of the world.

That did not mean that God was going to abrogate or terminate the first covenant. Instead, he would fill that covenant fuller. Moses and Elijah "spoke about his departure which he was about to *accomplish* in Jerusalem." It was to be a new and different kind of exodus. It would not be for saving people from the external bondage to Pharaoh, but from the internal bondage to selfishness and sin. It was the prophet Jeremiah through whom God promised a new day coming.

> "The time is coming when I will make a new covenant with the house of Israel. After that time I will put my law in their minds and write it on their hearts.....and I will forgive their wickedness and remember their sins no more. (Jeremiah 31:31)

I want you to notice that nothing is said here about *replacing* the first covenant. Why? It is because we use the word *new* in a number of ways. We replace an old carpet or worn out car and buy a new one. However "new" is not used that way here. Jesus nowhere says that. Instead, he said, "I did not come to destroy the law but to fulfill it." However, there are some in our time who believe what is called "replacement" theology. They say that those books of the Old Testament must be replaced as no longer relevant to our generation.

A recent controversy arose over this issue. It is a replay of the ancient controversy started by a man named Marcion in the early days of Christian history. Some people thought that it looked like

43

there were two different gods, the stern, judgmental, Old Testament God and the kind, loving forgiving God of the New Testament.

In present day America the issue has come up again. The Rev. Andy Stanley, pastor of a large non-denominational church in New Jersey, said that 'the Christian faith does not need to be propped up by the Jewish Scriptures, and in a post Christian context, our faith actually does better without old covenant support. Andy also said, "Christianity begins with Jesus, not Genesis." Jesus, however, did not simply appear out of thin air. He stands within the salvation history of Israel. Jesus had no intention of abrogating or replacing the first or Old Testament.

Later, Andy Stanley did "walk back" the disturbing comments he had made. He added that "the Old Testament is a kind of backstory. God was on the move in ancient times."[12] The implication is that He is not relevant to our high tech world of today. I am sure Andy does not really mean that.

So what should Andy have said? He should have recognized that in the Old Testament, *old* does not mean *age*, but *priority*. The coming of Jesus is not to be seen as a need to replace but *to fulfill* what God promised. By "new covenant or testament," we learn that the mission was still unfinished. It was for the Messiah, the Christ Jesus, to complete.

Next time you take part in a communion service, remember how the Old and New covenants are related. They are not related in the way that a worn out pair of shoes is replaced by a new pair, or an old car is replaced by a new one, but rather as a live theater where the Old Testament is Act One, and the New Testament is Act Two. Likewise, we do not begin to read mystery novels in the middle of the book. We do not enter a live theater when it is time for intermission and we have missed how the play has started.

Most of all, remember that there is one grand theme running through both Testaments. It is the coming into the world of the long

---

[12] Watson, David F, "Should we abandon the Old Testament?" *Good News*, Jan. 2019, p. 38

expected Messiah, Yeshua, Jesus of Nazareth, the one God sent as Savior of the world. He was not Jesus the Great, but Jesus the Only, the man with two natures, human and divine, who said,

"I have come that they might have life, and have it to the full." (John 10:10)

THE CRUCIFIXION

Cleopas and Mary must have been teary eyed as Jesus spoke of His crucifixion and death in such a matter-of-fact way. However, it was too hard for them to think about let alone go into detail of what they observed. As Jesus was suffering and dying, the chief priests and teachers of the law had mocked him, saying, "He saved others, but he can't save himself!" "Let this Christ, this king of Israel come down from the cross that we may see and believe!" They were asking for some supernatural intervention from God. However, as Jesus said before, it had to happen. Messiah died but he did not, could not, and would not stay dead. That was the grand finale, the resurrection that Cleopas and Mary had been learning about, a real time and space event. It was all according to the script God was following. Regardless of how it looked, everything was under His divine control.

QUESTIONS FOR DISCUSSION AND REFLECTION:

1. What are the dangers of moralism?
2. How can Jesus rightfully say that the Old Testament is all about him?
3. What is the proper relationship between the Old and the New Testaments?
4. What is the new exodus spoken of in the story of the Transfiguration?

CHAPTER SIX

Jesus Opens Eyes and Minds

It would be a great thing if we could rightly call Christians an incendiary fellowship of people with "burning hearts" set fire by the Holy Spirit. Out of gratitude to God, they are spreading the flames. If only that were as true for all as it is for many. Sometimes what hinders the expression of joy God gives are the cultural "brakes" which say that enthusiasm has its place but not in religion.

I grew up in a home where I felt loved by my parents, and where church going was expected. However, the unsaid rule was that we are to keep religious feelings to ourselves, and not "wear them on our sleeve." Solemnity, dignity and quiet devotion do have their place. Everything is to be done according to prescribed ritual. Exciting faith can seem like something unreal and fanatical. Yet there are times when genuine enthusiasm becomes uncontainable and too good to hold inside. Nonetheless, it should not become a distraction to others.

I think of a true story told to us seminary students in Cambridge, Massachusetts. In nearby Boston there is a large and famous Episcopal church where the mood at worship is prayerful silence unless there is congregational prayer or singing. Polite listening is the mode when the pastor is preaching.

On one occasion, the rector (senior pastor) was preaching when a middle-aged woman in a pew near the front started to wave her arms and shout "Hallelujah! and "Amen!" The pastor who told this story admitted that he did not know what to do, and just carried on as if nothing had happened. However, he said, a number of faces reflected their dislike of the woman's manners. This was at a formal and strictly traditional congregation: Trinity Church, Boston, no less! This outburst was considered nothing but a distraction. It was something that just was not done, especially there.

Finally, one of ushers walked down the main aisle to where the woman was seated alone. In a soft voice, he spoke near her ear and asked, "Madam, is anything wrong?" She spoke up loudly and said, "No, sir. Nothing's wrong. I've just got religion!" Not at all amused, he said to her, "Well! This is hardly the place for something like that!" She got up and left. He never saw her again. This is a true story. The rector himself told us.

This raises the issue. Is deep-seated joy and satisfaction in God's praise sometimes uncontainable? What about uncontainable joy at the football stadium? There you find cheerleaders helping fans express their feelings, not contain them.

What Cleopas and Mary experienced that first Easter afternoon was a degree of *uncontainable joy* that they felt deep inside as little by little Jesus explained the meaning of the Scriptures. They had followed Jesus for some time and found that there was something genuine and compelling about every one of his explanations. We can guess that their hands were gesturing often as the question/answer time came.

I know that this kind of fire in the mind and heart can and does happen but always in different ways depending on the context. It happened to me during my junior year in college when my own personal faith was, to use St. Paul's words, "fanned into flame." (2 Timothy 1:6) God used several clergy, a seasoned and very skilled preacher, a wise, discerning youth pastor, and a congregation of truly committed followers of Jesus to bring that same inner uncontainable joy. I simply had to know what made them different, what made their friendship so meaningful, their love for the Lord so apparent. What did they have that I lacked? What was their secret? The answer was the joy of being on the receiving end of undeserved grace from God. Once I realized the enormity of such a gift, everything else seemed very different. I had a new perspective.

Let us imagine for a moment that you are either Cleopas or his wife Mary. Jesus is choosing what and where he would begin to teach. Their seven-mile walk gave them plenty of time for this one- on- one kind of mentoring. For them it had to have been the eye opening experience of discovering where they were right, wrong, or confused. I can just hear them saying, "Oh, so that's what those words mean! Now I see!" They themselves said that as Jesus opened the eyes of their minds and understanding. This was the kindling which being lighted by the Holy Spirit was fanned into a heartwarming fire.

JESUS STARTED AT THE BEGINNING

A good guess is that Jesus started interpreting Scripture at the beginning, with Genesis chapter 1. There we read that God created ALL things including life in all forms, the human being of course as God's finest creation. Every human being reflects the image, the personality of God, with the ability to relate to Him and know Him. This is because humans, unlike animals, were given a soul, the part of us by which we relate and communicate with God. In fact, we are not bodies that have souls; we are souls that have bodies, as C.S. Lewis once put it.

Adam and Eve enjoyed a perfect relationship with their Maker until they made wrong choices and disobeyed God, thus breaking their relationship with Him and ending their right to live in a perfect environment called paradise.

Nonetheless, God revealed the merciful side of His personality. In Genesis 3:15 He hints that He will one day restore that broken relationship by doing something without any help from human beings. He would come into the world Himself as a human being, someone who would be a "seed," a descendant of the woman. This is a first clue: the seed is from the woman only and *not* from the man and the woman. God himself would be the father of a special child with two natures, one human and the other divine.

Jesus must have continued by referring Cleopas and Mary to the twelfth chapter of Genesis and the story of Abraham. It is the record of how God selected a man named Abram, the name used by family and friends in his hometown of Ur in ancient Iraq. Of all the people God might have chosen, He selected a man from a pagan family in a pagan country. Odd as it seems, Abram heard God's call and fully obeyed what God asked him to do. God was asking him to leave behind family, wealth and reputation. God did not say where He was taking Abram, but only that he would have to trust and obey.

Imagine the conversation between Abram and his wife, Sarah. "God said we have to move." "Where are we going, dear?" "I don't know." "Will we come back?" "I don't know." "What will we do there?" "I don't know." Like Abram, you and I still have to trust and obey, as the familiar hymn says.

Soon after this, God made Abram undergo a test. "Go take your son," God said, "the son you love, and offer him as a sacrifice on a mountain I will tell you about. (Genesis 22:2) Abram, coming from a pagan culture where such sacrifice was common, would not be surprised that God would make such a demand. It was all a test but Abram did not know that. Thus, he obeyed and went to a mountain where his young son Isaac consented to be sacrificed. Then, just a second before Abram was about to kill his son, an angel from God said, "Stop!" Abram looked and saw a ram caught in the bushes, and offered him as a substitute instead. That would be a foreshadowing and clue to the future time when Jesus would be our sacrifice and substitute. He made a covenant with him, saying that those who would bless Abraham would themselves receive a blessing and that Abraham's descendants would one day bless the whole world.

Abraham was father to Isaac, and Isaac to Jacob. Later in life when Jacob was pronouncing his final blessing to each of his twelve sons, Judah received a special promise. Judah would be the ancestor of a king, and the scepter, the symbol of royalty, would not depart from his line "until he comes to whom it belongs" (Gen.49:10). This was a promise that Messiah would eventually come from Judah's line and would be a king.

Perhaps Jesus went to Psalm 22, and to the very words that he spoke on the cross: "My God, my God, why have you forsaken me?" and other words about his hands and feet being pierced, and his clothes being divided up by lots as he died.

I am sure that as Cleopas and Mary walked along Jesus would also have gone to the prophet Daniel and read the famous story of the fiery furnace. It is a miracle story featuring a pagan king and a faithful Jew who would not bow down and worship an image of the king. Daniel and his friends were thrown into a blazing fire but the flames never touched them. In that fire was a mysterious fourth person standing next to the three Jews in the fiery furnace, the "one who looked like a son of the gods." (Daniel 3:25). Jesus explained that he was the fourth person in the fire, shielding him from harm and from thinking that God has deserted him. The king was amazed and rewarded Daniel and his friends.

Perhaps Jesus also went to Daniel 9:25 and to the prophecy of sixty-nine weeks of years, which would pass and add up exactly to the time when there would come a decree to rebuild the temple in Jerusalem in 30 A.D. That was the date when construction began.

I imagine he also went to Micah 5:2 where the prophet foretold the birth of the Messiah in Bethlehem of Judea:

> "But you, Bethlehem, Ephrathah, though you are small
> among the clans of Judah, out of you will come for me

one who will be ruler over Israel, whose origins are from of old, from ancient times."

Moving along, Jesus surely would have mentioned Zechariah 12:10 and the words of the prophet who said that one day Israel would "look on him whom they had pierced." No doubt, he also turned to Zechariah 9:9 where we read that Messiah would ride into Jerusalem on a donkey.

However, I am confident that the Isaiah passages would have given him the most to talk about. He might have started with the prophecy often read at Christmas.

> "The Lord himself will give you a sign: The virgin will be with child and will give birth to a son, and will call him Immanuel." (Isaiah 7:14)

Continuing with Isaiah, Jesus would have turned to chapter nine and these words:

> "For to us a child is born, to us a son is given, and the government will be upon his shoulders. And he will be called, Wonderful Counselor, Mighty God, Everlasting Father, Prince of Peace. Of the increase of his government and peace there will be no end. He will reign on David's throne and over his kingdom, establishing it and upholding it with justice and righteousness from that time on and forever." (Isaiah 9:6,7)

This means that Jesus, Messiah, would have a normal birth like yours and mine, but no beginning! His father would be God Himself!

Jesus must have spent some time on the most famous of all prophecies we know as the Suffering Servant passages:

> "Behold, my servant will prosper. He will be high and lifted up and greatly exalted, just as many were astonished at you, my people. So his appearance was marred more

than any man, and his form more than the sons of men."
(Isaiah 52:14)

Perhaps he would have gone on to Isaiah 53:2ff:

"His appearance would not attract us to him. He was
despised, forsaken of men, a man of sorrows, acquainted
with grief, despised, we didn't esteem him." "Surely he
took up our infirmities and carried our sorrows, yet we
considered him stricken by God, smitten by him, and
afflicted. But he was pierced for our transgressions, he
was crushed for our iniquities, and the punishment that
brought us peace was upon him, and by his wounds we
are healed. We all, like sheep, have gone astray, each of us
has turned to his own way; and the Lord has laid on him
the iniquity of us all." (Isaiah 53:4-6)

Note that Messiah's suffering was *for us,* as a *vicarious act*, done
in our place, not just in our behalf. This is the key to understand the
purpose of Jesus' coming into our world and dying on the cross.
What looked like a gross miscarriage of justice where an innocent
man was treated as guilty was really a voluntary giving of his life.
No one took his life; he laid it down. As he made clear to Governor
Pilate, God was in complete control. Had Jesus wanted he could
have called thousands of angels to his rescue, but he knew that the
scriptures had to be fulfilled.

To put it bluntly, that cross was meant for every human being.
That means it was for you and me. Jesus died in our place. He chose
the nails. He volunteered to make the supreme sacrifice because
human sin was that serious. God is holy and just. It would take
sinless person to qualify as Savior. No other human being but Jesus
qualified. The punishment had to be paid if a holy God could justly
forgive our sins. Here is how the apostle Peter put it:

"Christ died for sins, once for all, the righteous for the
unrighteous, to bring us to God." (1Peter 3:18)

That is the gospel in one sentence. Some theologians have called it "the glorious exchange." We trade our sins for Jesus' righteousness and our disobedience for his perfect obedience. In exchange, Jesus forgives our sin and offers us life everlasting.

These passages are only a few of many more we might call clues given by God in His long term plan of salvation As Cleopas and Mary listened to Jesus explain it, they were overcome with *awe and gratitude*. It is like a parent who says to a caregiver, "What you did for my child (or family member) is what you did for me."

Awesome, overwhelming gratitude and uncontainable joy is what fueled the fire in their hearts during that walk to Emmaus. Jesus so interpreted the Scriptures that they realized that they had really missed the central theme. Jesus had now resolved their misunderstanding about the purpose of Messiah's birth, death and resurrection. Their faith in God had been like smoldering coals. Now Jesus had fanned the coals into flames of gratitude and uncontainable joy.

Cleopas and Mary had now reached the turn that led to their home. Jesus, still unrecognized, acted as though he was going farther. The original Greek translates "pretend." This simply means that Jesus was politely waiting for Cleopas and Mary to say what they did. He did not ask to stay; he let them think he was going farther so that they would then invite him to their home for more teaching and fellowship. Perhaps he would be willing to spend the night with them. Travel was risky after dark, especially for a single person walking.

> "They drew near to the village to which they were going>
> Jesus acted as if he were going farther. *However, they
> urged him strongly, "Stay with us*, for it is nearly evening;
> the day is almost over." So he went in to stay with them"
> (Luke 24:29)

The wording, "stay with us" is very suggestive that Cleopas and Mary are talking about their own home, not an inn.

There, in the words of Cleopas and Mary, we have a pattern of what it takes to have Christ in our life. He always is a gentleman, always waits to be invited and never demands to be let in. He comes into the life of people who want him to come in and who urge him strongly to do so.

In front of me as I sit at my computer and type is the replica of a very large painting, which hangs in St. Paul's Cathedral, in London, England. It is a 25-foot high painting of the scene described in the Bible, Revelation 3:20, where Jesus is knocking on the door of a house. That house symbolizes our heart where Jesus wants to come in and be in close fellowship with us. The verse in Revelation says:

> "Here I am! I stand at the door and knock. If anyone hears
> my voice and opens the door, I will come in and eat with
> him and he with me." (Revelation3:20)

In the ancient world, the symbol of friendship and affection was the sharing of a meal together. This painting of Jesus knocking on the door is a message in art form. Jesus is waiting to be invited into our lives. By his knocking he is saying that he is available and willing to come in. This begs the question about you and me. Have we heard his knocking? Have we heard the knocking but decided not to answer and open the door for fear of being embarrassed or made to feel unworthy of his presence?

Or have we, like Cleopas, made it clear that we really do want him to stay? Just think what Cleopas and Mary would have missed if they had not urged him to come in.

> "When he was at the table he took bread, gave thanks,
> broke it and began to give it to them. Then their eyes were
> opened and the recognized him, and he disappeared from
> their sight."(Luke 24:31)

Notice that once again the passive voice is used, indicating the Spirit has lifted the veil from their eyes just as He had put it on them before. Is this scene supposed to remind Cleopas and Mary of the Last Supper experience? Some people think so. Even if they were not among the disciples in that upper room, perhaps they overheard or saw from outside the room what Jesus said and did during the ceremony. But there is no mention here of the Passover script as Jesus amended it.

Most likely, what Cleopas and Mary saw were the nail prints in Jesus hands as he lifted the broken bread in thanksgiving to God. Then Jesus opened their eyes in the same way he had closed them when he came looking for them. Then they recognized him. Imagine their surprise and their amazement! Remember that they had watched the crucifixion only hours before. Words fail us when we try to describe such an impossible surprise! Then he disappeared, yet he did not leave them. *He only became invisible and they could no longer see him.*

> "They asked each other, "Were not our hearts burning within us while he talked with us on the road and opened the Scriptures to us? They got up and returned at once to Jerusalem." (Luke 24:33)

Even though it was dark and late, they were willing to take risks with their own safety. The news of resurrection was that exciting and had to be told.

Do you realize what this means to us? *It means that Jesus is with us even when we cannot see him.* The resurrection of Jesus made that possible.

William Frey, a retired bishop of the Episcopal Church, Diocese of Colorado, tells of the time many years ago when he volunteered to read to an older student named John, who was totally blind. On one occasion, he asked John, "How did you lose your eyesight?" "I was thirteen," he replied, "and there was a chemical explosion." Bishop Frey asked, "How did that make you feel?" John replied, with total honesty, "I felt like my life was over. I hated God. For the first six months, I did nothing but stay in my room, all alone. I would eat all by myself, by my choice. Then the weather changed and a curious thing happened. One day my father entered the room and said, "John, winter's coming and the storm windows need to be put on. That is your job. I want the storm windows hung by the time I get back this evening or else." Then John's father turned and walked out of the room and slammed the door. By now, John was so angry that he was thinking, "Who does he think he is? Who does he think I am? I am *blind!*"

He was so furious that he actually decided to try to install the storm windows for selfish reasons. "I am going to show them. I am going to try to do it, and I am going to be not only blind but paralyzed, because I am going to fall. I'll show them!" So he slowly felt his way to the garage and found the storm windows and all the necessary tools.

John found the ladder, and all the while, he was muttering under his breath: "I will show them. I will fall and they will have a blind and paralyzed son. That will be great payback." Eventually, though, he did complete the job, and he did not fall. He got the windows up before evening. However, this assignment achieved more than that. It achieved the father's goal as well. John reported that it was at that point that he slowly realized that he could still work, and even more so, that he could begin to reconstruct his life. As John continued to tell Bishop Frey his story, John's eyes, his blind eyes, began to mist. "Seven years later, I learned that something else important had happened that day. I learned *that the entire day my father was no more than three or four feet from me!*"[13]

This reminds me of a great promise of Jesus about the work of the Holy Spirit. He is not seen, but is always as close as blind John was to his father.

> "The Counselor, the Holy Spirit, whom the Father will send in my name, will teach you all things and remind you of everything I said to you." "If anyone loves me he will obey my teaching. My Father will love him, and we will come to him and make our home with him." (John 14:23,26)

---

[13] Frey, William, *Dance of Hope*, Colorado Springs, Co. Waterbrook Press, 2003

QUESTIONS FOR DISCUSSION AND REFLECTION:

1. What role does the Holy Spirit play in helping us interpret what we read in the Scriptures?
2. Why can't God just forgive and forget? Why the cross?
3. What is meant by the glorious exchange?
4. If you could have been with Cleopas and Mary what questions would you have wanted to ask Jesus?

CHAPTER SEVEN

The Strangely Warmed Heart

T he story of John Wesley, founder of Methodism, can help us further understand this compelling metaphor of hearts "on fire."

John Wesley lived in the mid 1700's in England. He was the son of a Church of England pastor, and was educated at Oxford University. Following a period of training under his father, he applied for ordination to the Anglican priesthood. He wrote in his journal that his formal religious education was mainly intellectual. He was "strictly educated and taught that people could only be saved by keeping the commandments, by being not as bad as other people, by reading the Bible, by saying prayers and by attending church." However, I wonder if he was exaggerating a bit to make his point.

We know this familiar approach as *moralism.* It is about being good, doing good, and thereby trying to earn God's favor. Such faith is the attempt to save ourselves by our own good works. There is no converted, submitted heart that shows gratitude for God's unmerited love. It is instead a climbing of the ladder of good deeds, but never knowing how many more rungs there are to climb. This great man, who was to go on to become the leader of the Methodist revival in England and beyond, experienced a total spiritual makeover.

Wesley signed on to a mission work in the colony of Georgia in America with special intention of evangelizing the Native Americans. On arriving, he met a Moravian (similar to Lutheran) pastor who had a deep Biblical faith in Jesus Christ. This pastor asked Wesley "Do you know Jesus Christ?" Wesley replied, "I know that he is savior of the world." "Yes," the pastor said, "but do you know that he saved you?" Wesley said, "I hope he has died to save me." Notice John's hesitation to say yes, and his uncertain faith.

That lack of assurance haunted him. It no doubt lessened his effectiveness when trying to evangelize the Indians. He actually wrote in his Letters, that his chief motive in going to the Indians was the hope of saving his own soul.

After about two years in Georgia, Wesley returned to England and sought further advice from the newly organized Moravian societies in London. A man named Peter Bohler helped him learn the meaning of genuine "saving faith" such as Luther had preached it, that Christ literally took our place and died for our sins on the cross. Wesley discovered that the only thing we can contribute to that process is the very sin from which we all need to be rescued.

The turning point was Wesley's attendance at an evening Moravian service on Aldersgate St. in London. The local pastor was preaching on Luther's commentary on the book of Romans, and the change that God works through saving faith in Christ. Various words have been used to describe what happened that night. Some say conversion, others a personal revival or transformation, but whatever it was, the result of it was, in Wesley's words, like a "stony heart being melted down and made into soft, tender flesh." For him obedience took on a new motivation. He was no longer to trust and obey because he needed to prove his faith, but now his obedience to God's law was his way of loving God back for loving him. His motivation became an overwhelming desire to show God his gratitude for God's undeserved grace and mercy revealed by Jesus Christ.

What do we mean when we say grace and mercy? Mercy is God *not giving us* the judgment our sins deserve; grace is God *giving us* the forgiveness we do not deserve. This great gift of God is what John Wesley knew about from his training at Oxford, but he had never actually received himself. Then, as he was sitting and listening to the preacher at the church on Aldersgate St., spiritual flames broke out in his heart. That is when the impersonal and academic truth about Jesus became personal, intrinsic and uniquely his own. He knew that Christ was savior of the world, but more than that, he now realized that Christ died for John Wesley.

"One was reading Luther's preface to the Epistle to the Romans. At about a quarter to nine while he was describing the change that God works in the heart through faith in Christ, I felt *my heart strangely warmed.* I felt I did trust in Christ, Christ alone for salvation, and an assurance was given me that he had taken away my sins, EVEN MINE, and saved me from the law of sin and death." [14]

He was a new person whose identity was now in Christ. To use the contrast of Ezekiel the prophet, his heart changed from stone to flesh. His faith in Christ changed formal, orthodox Anglican doctrine into repaired relationships, new motivations, priorities, with a focus on the person of Christ.

This is not something like loud cheers for a football team winning the Super Bowl. This is not the "fire in the belly" we think of when describing a politician campaigning for votes. This is not the high emotion and elation felt when the votes are in and all the supporters of the winner celebrate with fireworks, balloon drops, and other expressions of joy. No, the "strangely warmed heart" is one where we ponder deeply what it means to experience God's undeserved and unlimited grace.

Wesley was well read in his theological studies, and the doctrine of the atonement of Christ would have been a cherished truth for

---

[14] Goodnewsmag.org/2017/07/strangely warmed

him. However, by his own admission, such great doctrines remained academic, external, and impersonal. Then that time came when it became personal, and wonderfully internalized. Before Aldersgate, Wesley did not have assurance of his salvation. He thought of himself as an "Almost Christian" but now he said he was an "Altogether Christian." Saving faith is not a speculative, rational, intellectual assent, a train of ideas in the head but it is also a disposition of the heart. It is a full reliance on the blood of Christ, and a trust in the merits of his life, death and resurrection.

Why then was Aldersgate Street so important in Wesley's Christian life? For the same reason it is important in your life and mine. The purpose of Christ's coming into the world was to change the world by changing people, *one at a time*. If we see no need for that costly sacrifice on the cross for our sins, then we are in fact still trying to save ourselves by trying to be good.

Moralism is no more helpful to us than it was to John Wesley. We need to see that our salvation is not mostly a gift and partly a reward. It is all grace, not mostly grace and some good works on our part. There are no other options. "For by grace you have been saved and that not of yourselves. It is the gift of God not of works, lest anyone boast." (Ephesians 2:7-9)

As Luther put it, we are saved by faith alone, by grace alone, by Christ alone, but not by faith that *is alone*. Being good and doing good is way of saying thank you to God for what He did for us, not for deserving our salvation. By the cross we exchange our sins for Jesus' righteousness, our disobedience for his perfect obedience. This is the way to saving faith, the change from John Wesley's "Almost Christian" into the "Altogether Christian." It is the only way to gain the assurance we want from God.

The burning heart stands for much more than a feeling that comes from happy surprises. We are talking about something so deep and real that it changes our priorities all around until nothing in our busy lives becomes more important than treasuring Christ above all else. That relationship is not for sale, nor can we do anything for God or give Him anything of ours to get it. We cannot fool Him. He knows our motivations. He can see through our efforts to please Him in order to get something out of him.

Here is the point: It is all too easy to be *selfish* in our unselfishness. The remedy is not easy but it is simple. We need to want *God* more than we want anything *from* God. Cleopas and Mary needed to realize that. We are to serve Him not to get something but to thank Him for something. The truth is that there is nothing we can give that is not already His. All giving to Him, is giving back. All loving Him is loving back. In many churches when the morning offering is presented to the pastor the congregation says:

> "All things come of thee, O Lord, and of thine own have
> we given thee." (1 Chronicles 29:14)

Perhaps it is because some of us in Anglicanism hear this every week that we miss the profound meaning of it. It means that we own *nothing* of what we possess. Everything is on loan from God who made us and everything else for our needs. We really own nothing, even our bodies themselves. We simply give God back a portion of what He gave us. This insight must have been part of the eye opening and heartwarming experience on the walk with Jesus to Emmaus. This is the meaning of a key verse in the Old Testament:

> "You may say to yourself, "My power and the strength of
> my hands have produced this wealth for me." But remember
> the Lord your God, for it is he who gives you the ability to
> produce wealth, and so confirms his covenant, which he
> swore to your forefathers, as it is today." (Deuteronomy
> 8:17, 18)

The historical tradition of the centuries is clear; the Scriptures are what God says they are, namely His written word.

Quite simply we submit to the authority of Scripture because we submit to the authority of Christ. Remember that Jesus did not give Scripture authority. It already had and still has the authority of God Himself.

As I was reading and rereading this story of the walk to Emmaus, I remembered the time at the beginning of his ministry when he was in prayer with the Father and thinking how his ministry should begin. As he was pondering this, Satan appeared in human disguise, with offers to "help" Jesus gain followers. "Turn stones to bread," Satan suggested. "Jump off the temple roof" and onlookers would be impressed. The last of the temptations must have had the most appeal to anyone but Jesus. "Bow down and worship me," Satan said, "and I will give you all the kingdoms of the world." Satan was breaking a famous rule that we cannot do evil in a good cause. We do not consult the enemy for advice in how to defeat him.

Jesus simply replied and quoted Scripture. God's authority behind His written word was reason enough to refuse. Satan had no comeback or debate. He simply changed the temptation and tried again. Here is my point: If you and I are living under the authority of Christ as his followers then our attitude toward Scripture must be the same as his. Remember how he said:

> "A servant is not above his master; it is enough for a servant to be like his master and a student to be like his teacher."(Matthew10:24)

Such a statement is truly counter-cultural and counter-intuitive. Jesus asks us to take on a servant role whereas the culture models for us the self-centered role. Many Christians chafe under the demand of Jesus to reverse the natural and human tendency to put self first. Humility is one of the virtues of the Christian life most unlike the values that the world admires. This makes it a difficult challenge.

THE STAGECOACH LESSON

Back in the American Wild West days, the stagecoach was a main means of transportation. At the most, the vehicle carried six passengers. Yet even with so few passenger space the practice of going first, second and third class was followed. The difference had nothing to do with the size of the seat or whether or not any food was served, but what was expected of the ticket holder in case the stagecoach became stuck in the mud or was too heavy for the horses to pull up a hill.

First class tickets were the most expensive, of course, and they entitled the ticket holders to remain inside the coach no matter what the conditions outside. This meant that they were not expected to put forth any effort in getting the coach out of difficulty. A second-class ticket meant that they had to get out, lighten the weight and walk alongside the coach until the problem was resolved. The cheapest ticket, the third class, called on the ticket holder to take responsibility for getting the coach back in service. Along with the driver, they were required to help get the coach out of the mud or up the hill. Third class tickets required a willingness to do whatever it took to serve in time of need. There was no place for pride.

As I thought about the practice of Wells Fargo with passengers, it reminded me of how different the values of Jesus are from those of the culture. In fact, Jesus turned such values upside down and right side up. In his eyes, first class was opposite from being exempt from the role of a servant, and excused from any unpleasant but necessary work. In the ethic of the kingdom of God, everyone looks for ways to serve, not to avoid them. A servant thinks of how they can help, not how others might help them. *This means that God's first class is the world's third class.* People in this class already have their need for approval and acceptance met by the unearned grace of God. Since those needs are already met, Christians no longer need to prove that they are better than anyone else is. Humility reminds us that the only person we need to please is Jesus. We do that by being like him, not the successful man or woman our culture holds up for us to admire.

There is nothing dated about this reversal of values Jesus came to model. This is something everyone can understand and practice in any generation. We cannot update it or upgrade it by pointing out the differences between the ancient world and the high tech culture we are living in now.

Mark Twain's comment comes to mind: "It's not the parts of the Bible that I don't understand that I don't like; what I don't like are parts of the Bible that I *do* understand!" So many issues up for discussion today appear to be issues never seen before. However, when we dig deeper into those issues we find that the issue is an old one wearing a contemporary disguise.

It is strange how those seven deadly sins just never go away. I remember them by the word "salvage." Sloth, avarice, lust, vanity, anger, greed and envy. They are timeless. This is why the gospel is never outdated, and why Jesus' gospel is always relevant. It is why every part of the Scripture is in some degree the record of how God was unveiling His plan of salvation even from page one of Genesis. How true it is that Jesus found references to himself in all of the Old Testament.

How could Cleopas and Mary *not* have fire in their hearts when they realized that their new hope was their trust in a Redeemer so great that he could die and rise again? His plan of redemption was so much better than theirs, and it was than a plan in God's mind since all eternity!

Listen to Paul as he puts this joy into his own words. He is writing to the Christians in Thessalonica, near present day Greece.

> "And we also thank God continually because when you received the word of God, which you heard from us, you accepted it not as the word of men, but as it actually is, the word of God, which is at work in you who believe." (I Thessalonians 2:13)

Notice the tense of the verb: It is "the word of God which IS at work in you who believe." It is about Jesus but not just the past. It is correspondence from him through words written long ago but with a message for you and me NOW."

The Scripture does contain a lot of history of the Jewish people and later of the people who followed Jesus and started Christianity. However, much more than this, the Scripture is written in such a way as always to be fresh and applicable to every generation of believers.

Cleopas and Mary changed their minds completely about redeeming Israel. Now their wish for the end of Roman occupation had given way to a totally new kind of prayer. Now they prayed that the desires of Jesus become identical with theirs. It is like praying "thy kingdom come," as you are thinking to yourself, "and my kingdom go!"

I believe that this is what was happening in the minds of this couple on the road to Emmaus. Previously they had been following Jesus from place to place, learning, admiring, respecting and even believing the claims of Jesus, but without the assurance the resurrection gave them. What he was saying is that if we are not careful we will love *the means* more than the end. So easily we can be busy with "oiling the machine" of the church, as one clergy friend put it recently, that we forget why we are doing what we do. We can so easily make good things into ultimate things, and when we do that, we create an idol and we worship it instead of God.

A highly respected and elder Episcopal bishop was addressing a group of us clergy. In his speech he said, "I have to confess to you with some embarrassment and shame that I have sometimes been more in love with the Church than with the Lord of the Church." You could have heard a pin drop. All of us clergy resonated with what he was saying. If we are not careful, whatever we treasure the most, apart from God, even our ordained ministry, can become an idol and a counterfeit God.

What Jesus showed Cleopas and Mary that first Easter was that he, Jesus, is both the means and the end. He is the subject of all the Scripture, both Testaments, First and Second, (Old and New). Everything is about him! And he is alive!

QUESTIONS FOR DISCUSSION AND REFLECTION:

1. Why can't we update, upgrade or make the Scriptures more geared to the times we are living in?
2. In what ways can a good thing become a real idol?
3. In what ways are we tempted to be better or different from our Master?

CHAPTER EIGHT

The Moonwalk and the Jesus Walk

L ast year, 2019, marked the fiftieth anniversary of an actual
walk that will go down in history as the day when something
impossible actually happened. It was the landing of an
American made spacecraft on the moon, July 20, 1969.

Our imagination gave way to pure human history when the
television showed the actual landing. However, some who were
watching from the earth doubted if it was real. Perhaps, they thought,
it was only a well-rehearsed stunt filmed in some remote desert. Now,
when someone says that to Brig. Gen. Charles (Charlie) Duke, who
actually walked on the moon in a later mission, he replies, "Do you
think that if it were fake we would have done it over?" Yes, it really
happened.

Imagine a fraternity of men, which at its founding had ten people
in it but now has only four living members. The reason is that to be
a member you have to be someone who has literally walked on the

moon and returned safely to earth! Actually there really is such a fraternity and I have had the privilege of meeting Gen. Duke, a now world famous astronaut. He became the 10th, and youngest, person to walk on the moon during the Apollo Mission 16 in 1972. "Charlie" was part of Mission Control in Houston during the first trip to the moon 1969. Astronaut Neil Armstrong was the first human being to step onto the moon. We remember Armstrong saying, as he landed from the lunar landing vehicle, "One small step for man, one giant leap for mankind."

Later in 1972, Charlie Duke had the privilege of spending three days in the exploration of the lunar surface and riding in the space vehicle across the rocky terrain. There are no clouds over the moon and neither is there any atmosphere. Astronauts bring their own air.

On his way to the moon, Charlie was able to peer through the window of the capsule and look back at the earth. Putting his hand under the blue marble earth seen in the window, he could make the song come alive: "He's got the whole world in his hands." At the same time, he realized that at that moment on the journey he was actually more than 20,000 miles from home! Yet in some ways, he was even farther away from God.

However, he would say to you now, the much more important walk began almost exactly seven years later. Charlie had grown up in a church but he never knew what he was missing. He did not have a personal relationship with Jesus as Savior and Lord. Later however he discovered what it was. The change began to take place when he and his wife attended a three-day parish retreat called "Faith Alive." The weekend finished with a challenge to evaluate whether or not those in attendance knew what it meant to make a personal commitment to Christ as Lord. Charlie's wife did and changes in her life became obvious to him. He knew that he needed what she had and, just as it was true for his walk on the moon, his walk with Jesus started with small steps. It took about six full years from when he walked on the moon to when he started walking with the Lord. He started to read the Bible with a new interest. "I began to devour Scripture, several hours a day, and the more I read, the more conviction the Lord brought upon me. "God delivered me from anger, unforgiveness, just everything that was wrong. He saved our marriage. Not one promise of God has failed us."

Sometimes he laughs at the irony of it all. "People all over the world want to meet someone who has walked on the moon. But all I want is to introduce them to the only perfect Person to walk on the earth."

Please permit me to ask if you, the reader, have been introduced to that perfect Person, the man who made the much longer and different kind of journey from heaven to earth. He was and is God in the flesh, the man who was both human and divine, the one who would remove your sins and mine, even though it meant dying on the cross, paying our sin debt in full, all to express his undeserved and unlimited love and acceptance. Do you want Jesus to give you what he gave to Cleopas and Mary, the ultimate gift of hearts on fire with uncontainable joy?

In the past 40 years, Charlie has spoken all over the world about his walk on the moon and about his impersonal belief in God whom he was trying to please by doing good things. That was pure moralism, a kind of self-salvation by trying to earn and deserve the favor of God. He had not yet surrendered control of his life to Christ as Lord and Savior. As a result, he had no peace inside. He now knows why at that time his marriage and family life were, as he puts it, "in shambles." His career became his idol and his marriage suffered from it.

Then, in 1975, his church in Texas offered a weekend experience in reviving and renewing faith. *Faith Alive* is a nondenominational ministry, which gives those who attend a fresh look at the person and work of Christ. In addition, the team of Faith Alive brings testimonies from those who have found new life and hope through their commitment to Christ as Lord and Savior.

It is what I call the "satisfied customer" approach to sharing our faith with those who are not yet committed believers. A satisfied customer in the business world is someone who has heard praise for a certain product, perhaps on television or the internet, or from a neighbor or friend, and then goes out and buys it to see if the claims are true.

As we all know, there is no better way to test a claim than to hear what another person says and then test its truth for ourselves. As a former member of the national board of *Faith Alive,* I joined with other members and provided the weekend experience for my own congregation. Then I helped in setting up the program for congregations elsewhere. The good news is that many people are truly enthusiastic about the weekend and come away from it with a new and meaningful faith in Jesus Christ. It was the weekend at Charlie's church that made it personal. Dotty Duke was the first to profit from it.

After her commitment to Jesus as Lord and Savior, her sadness turned into joy. Charlie, however, needed more time. He needed more time to learn that there are no substitutes for Christ. He thought at first that his happiness might come in other ways. He thought that the happiness he was seeking might come from running first one and then several new businesses. However, running those businesses did not bring him the peace he was seeing in Dotty. Then he realized that God was custom designing just the right opportunity for him.

Sometimes God chooses to work that way. He allows us to experience disappointment to make us ready to commit to Christ in His time and in His way. When we learn that "my way" is not working, we are ready for other ways. Perhaps our answer comes through trial and error, or a process of elimination, as was true in my case.

A doctor friend in a nearby town invited Charlie to a Bible study at his ranch. Charlie went, but only because of the doctor's friendship. This time God had his attention. It seemed as though God were asking him to make up his mind about Jesus. He felt that he had to choose to accept Jesus' offer to bring peace and satisfaction to those who would say yes and really mean it. He sat in his car that Sunday afternoon after the Bible study ended, and made the commitment to put Jesus first in his life. Finally the peace came, along with a desire for more of the gospel truth. Slowly but surely he learned that Jesus

Christ could be trusted, and had the answers to what was missing in his life.

Charlie has been walking now to another Emmaus, not the address in Luke 24 which is seven miles west of Jerusalem, nor in the hill country of Texas where he lives, but to the address in the hill country of his soul. He is always ready to say that although his walk on the moon was incredibly exciting and meaningful, his life long walk with Jesus is far better.

Here is how Charlie expressed it: "I used to say that I could live ten thousand years and never have an experience as thrilling as walking on the moon. But the excitement and satisfaction of that walk doesn't begin to compare with my walk with Jesus, a walk that lasts forever."

Not everybody has the chance to walk on the moon but everybody has the opportunity to walk with the Son. It cost billions of dollars to send someone to the moon, but walking with Jesus is free, although in another sense it "costs" everything. We have to surrender everything to the Lord's control. Charlie said, "You don't need to go to the moon to find God. I found Him on the front seat of my car on Highway 46 in New Braunfels, Texas when I opened my heart to Jesus. And my life hasn't been the same since."[15]

As I conclude our study of the walk to Emmaus, I have several prayers for you.

Like John Wesley, I pray that you will take in the awesome truth that Christ *died for you, even you.*

Like Charlie Duke, I pray that every day will seem like a personal surrender of everything to the Lord Jesus and his control.

Like Cleopas and Mary, I pray that Christ will open the eyes of your heart and mind to see how all the promises of God are filled and filled fuller in him.

Here is a poem which frames our thoughts about the cross and resurrection of Christ. I close with it and pray that you want your heart to be on fire. It is part of an English hymn that promises that

---

[15] Duke, Charles, Moonwalker:, Nashville, Tn. Oliver Nelson, 1990, p. 280

God's love that will burn in our hearts when we realize the depths of God's love for us. His love is our incentive for wanting to show our gratitude by loving Him back.

"I sometimes think about the cross

And shut my eyes and try to see

The cruel nails and crown of thorns

And Jesus crucified for me

But even could I see him die

I could but see a little part

Of that great love which like a fire

Is always burning in my heart" [16]

---

[16] William W. How, "It is a Thing Most Wonderful", public domain

Printed in the United States
By Bookmasters